THIS BOOK BELONGS TO:

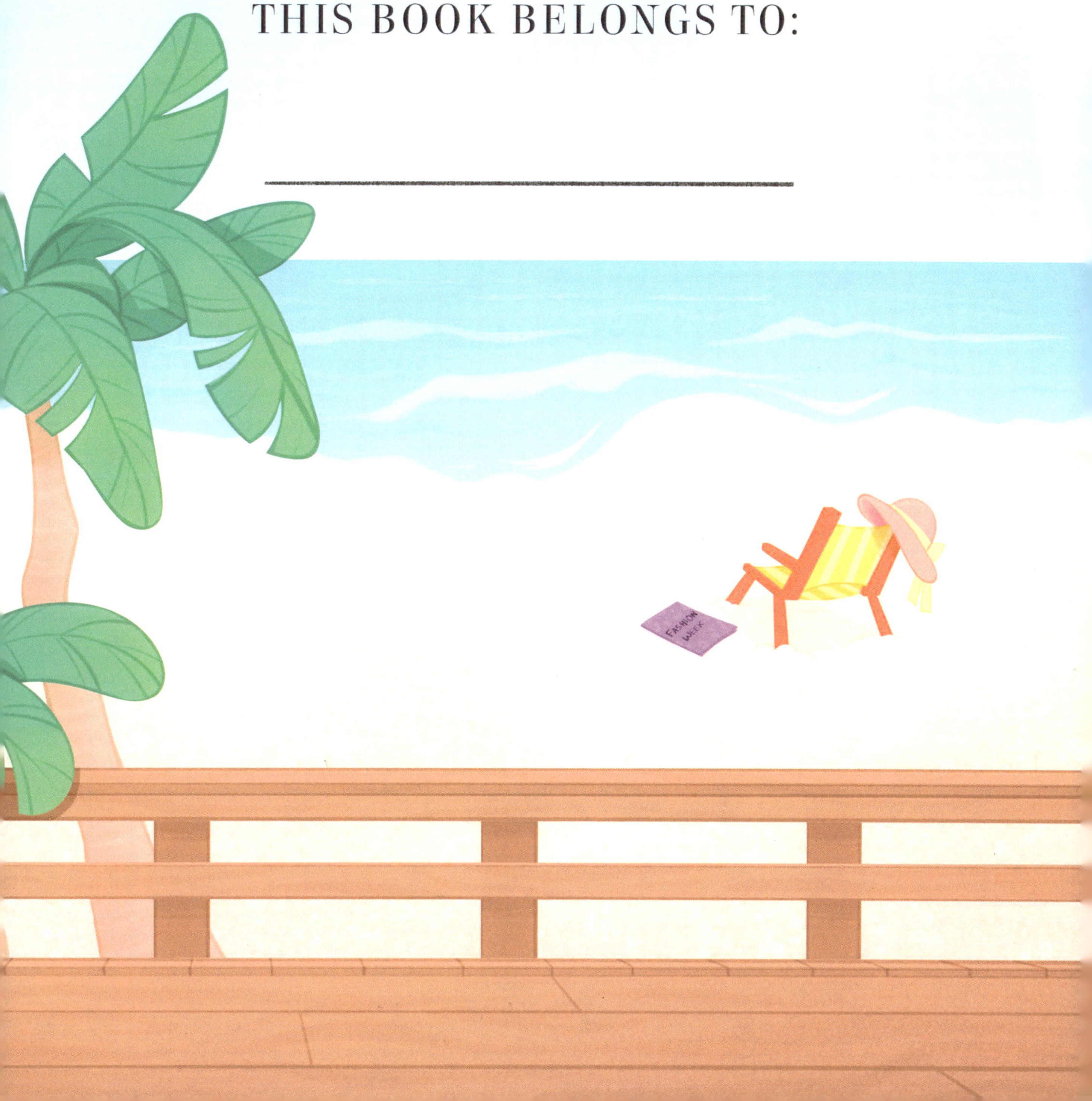

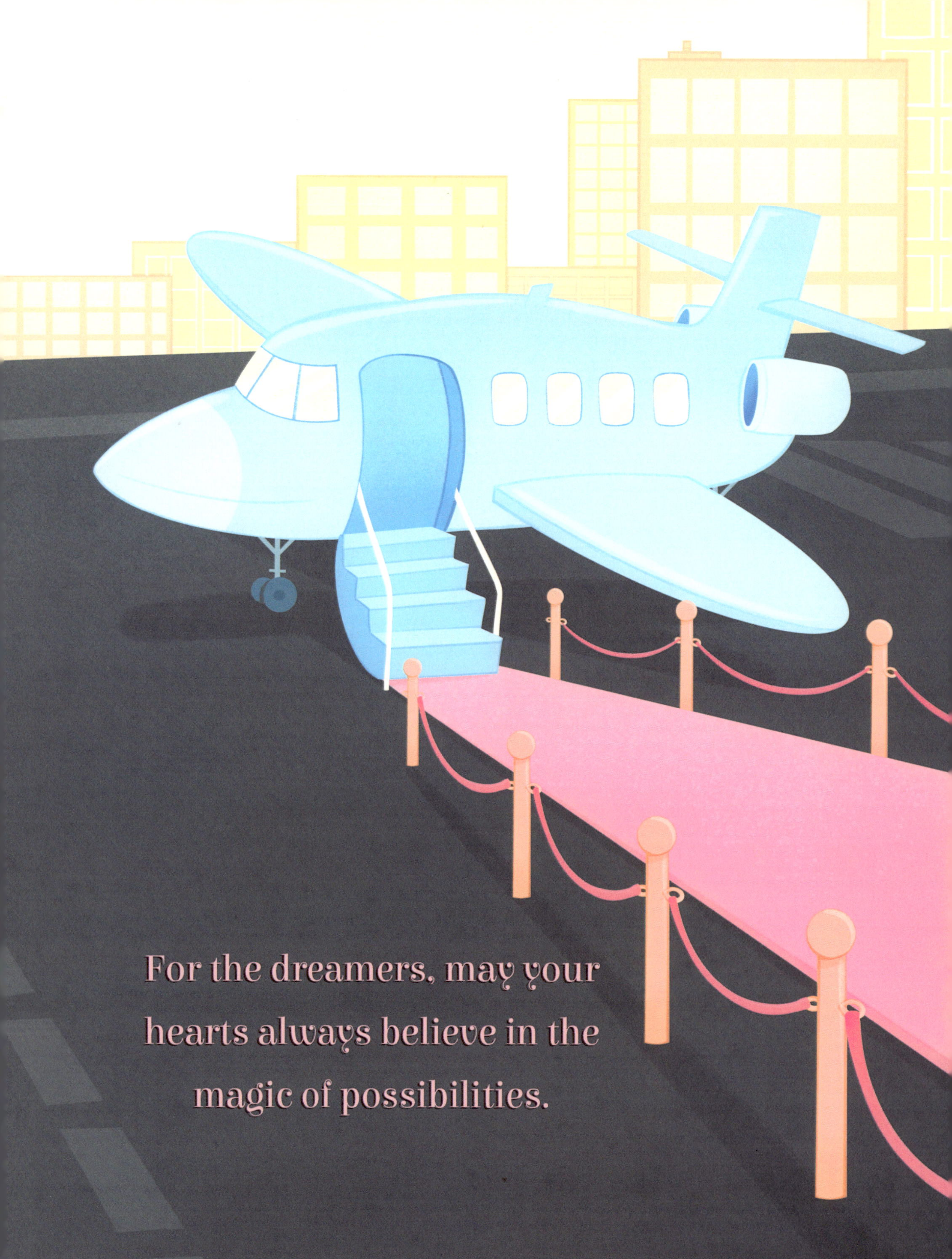

For the dreamers, may your hearts always believe in the magic of possibilities.

Farrah the Fashionista: Miami Swim Week

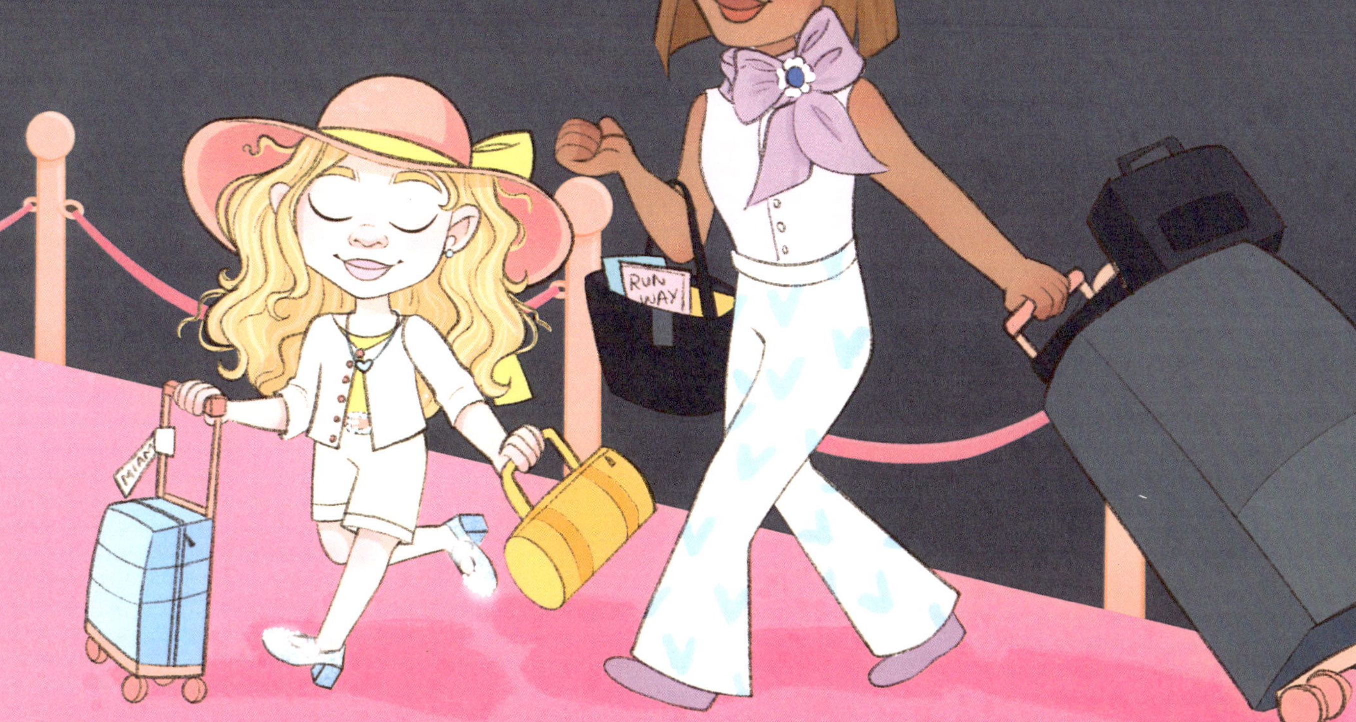

written by
Amy Gentry-Tabb

illustrated by
Hayley Blackwood

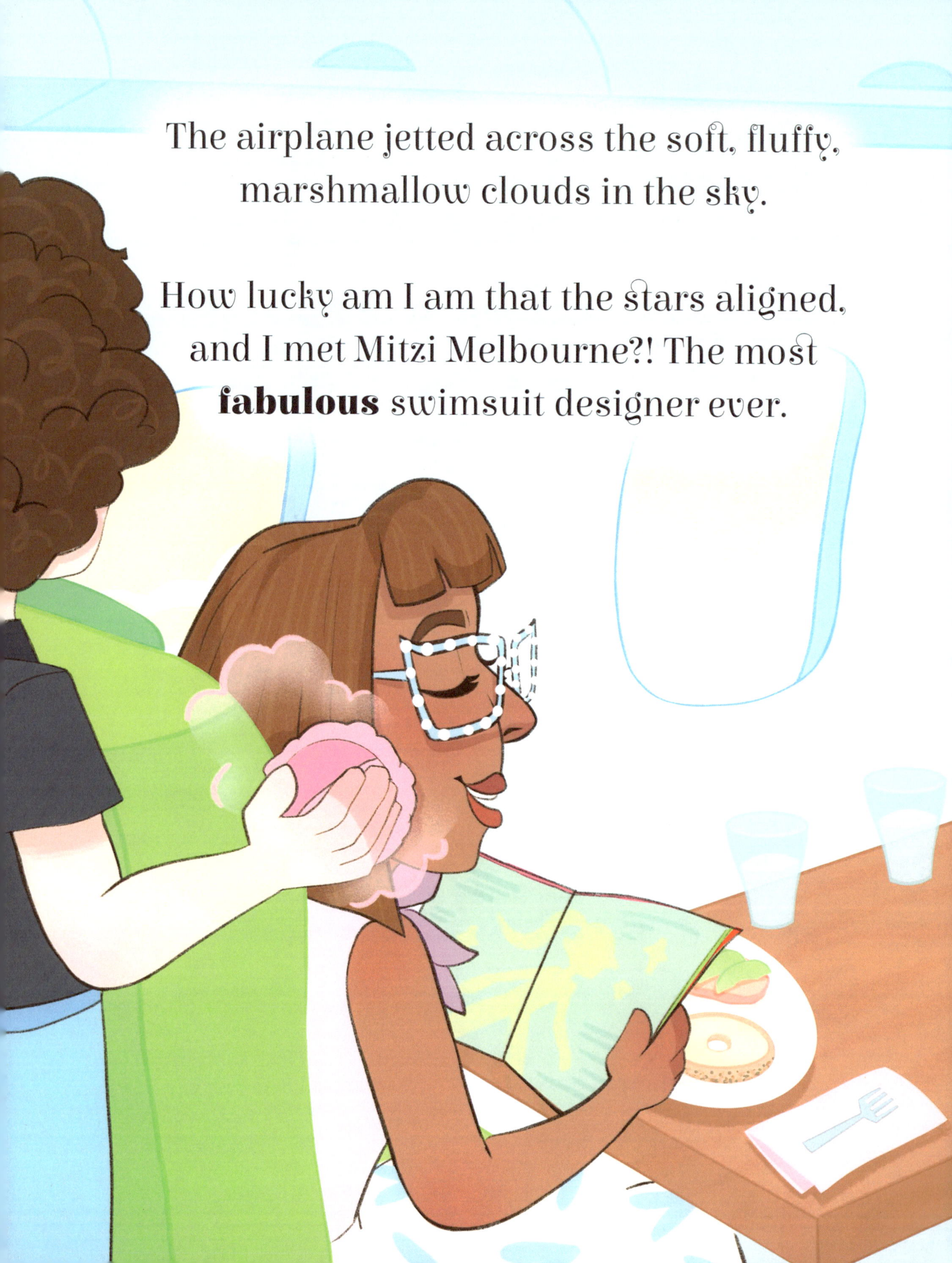

The airplane jetted across the soft, fluffy, marshmallow clouds in the sky.

How lucky am I am that the stars aligned, and I met Mitzi Melbourne?! The most **fabulous** swimsuit designer ever.

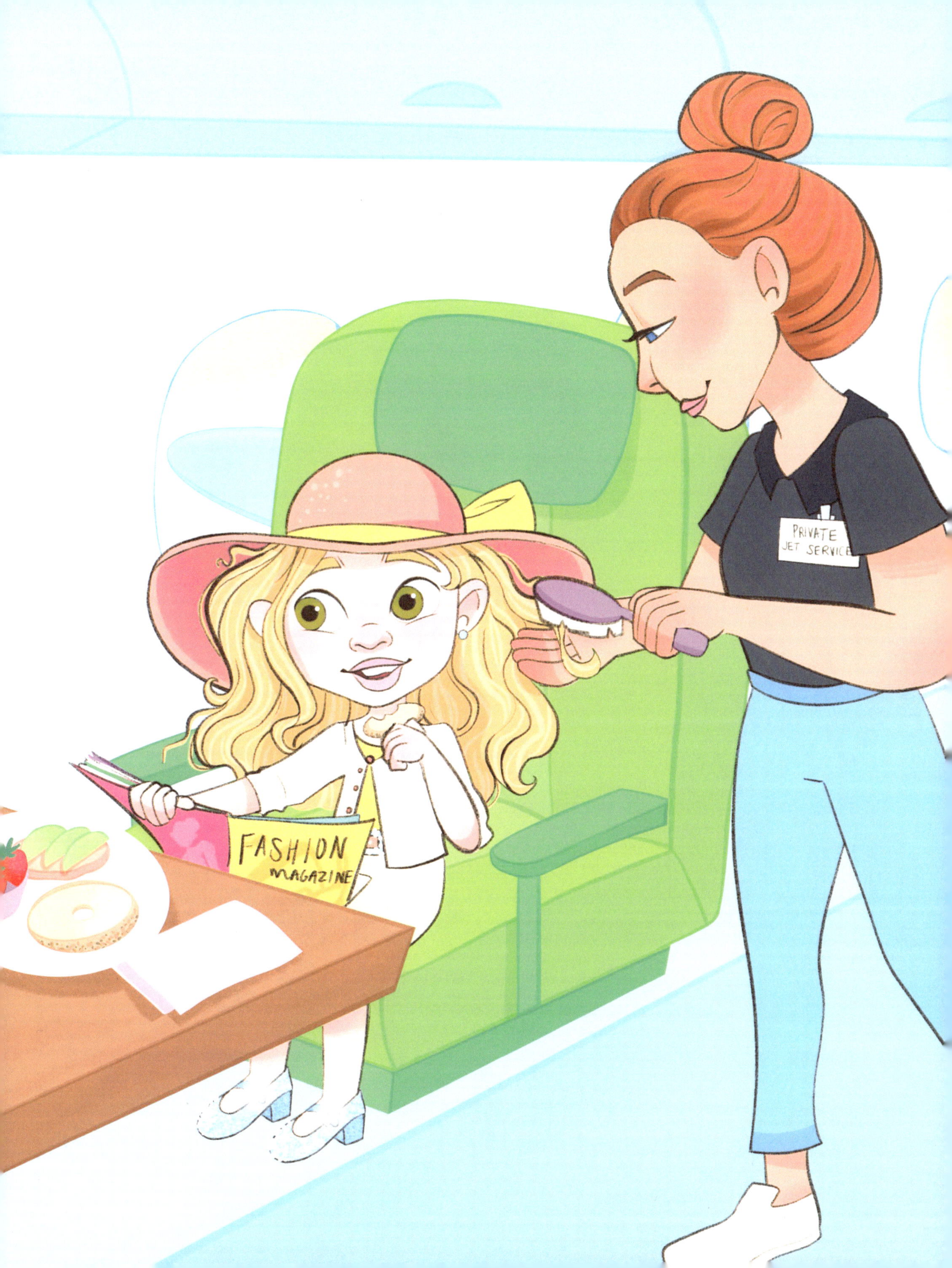

FASHION
MAGAZINE
PRIVATE
JET SERVICE

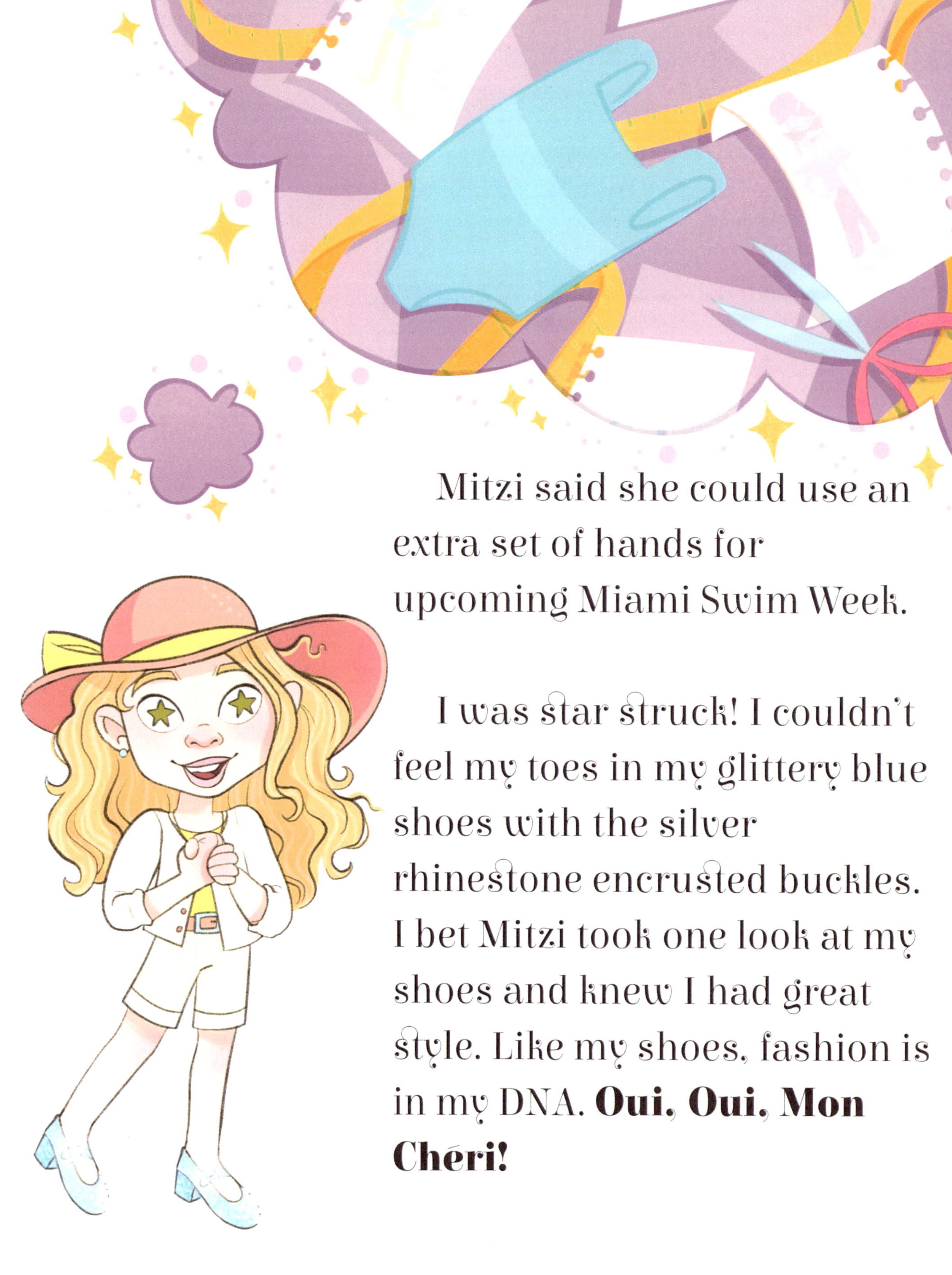

Mitzi said she could use an extra set of hands for upcoming Miami Swim Week.

I was star struck! I couldn't feel my toes in my glittery blue shoes with the silver rhinestone encrusted buckles. I bet Mitzi took one look at my shoes and knew I had great style. Like my shoes, fashion is in my DNA. **Oui, Oui, Mon Chéri!**

"Farrah, I love your energy, enthusiasm, and style. You have 'fashion hustle,' and I admire it! You are just what I am looking for," she said.

I was going to rock the runway show as "**THE**" assistant to Mitzi Melbourne.

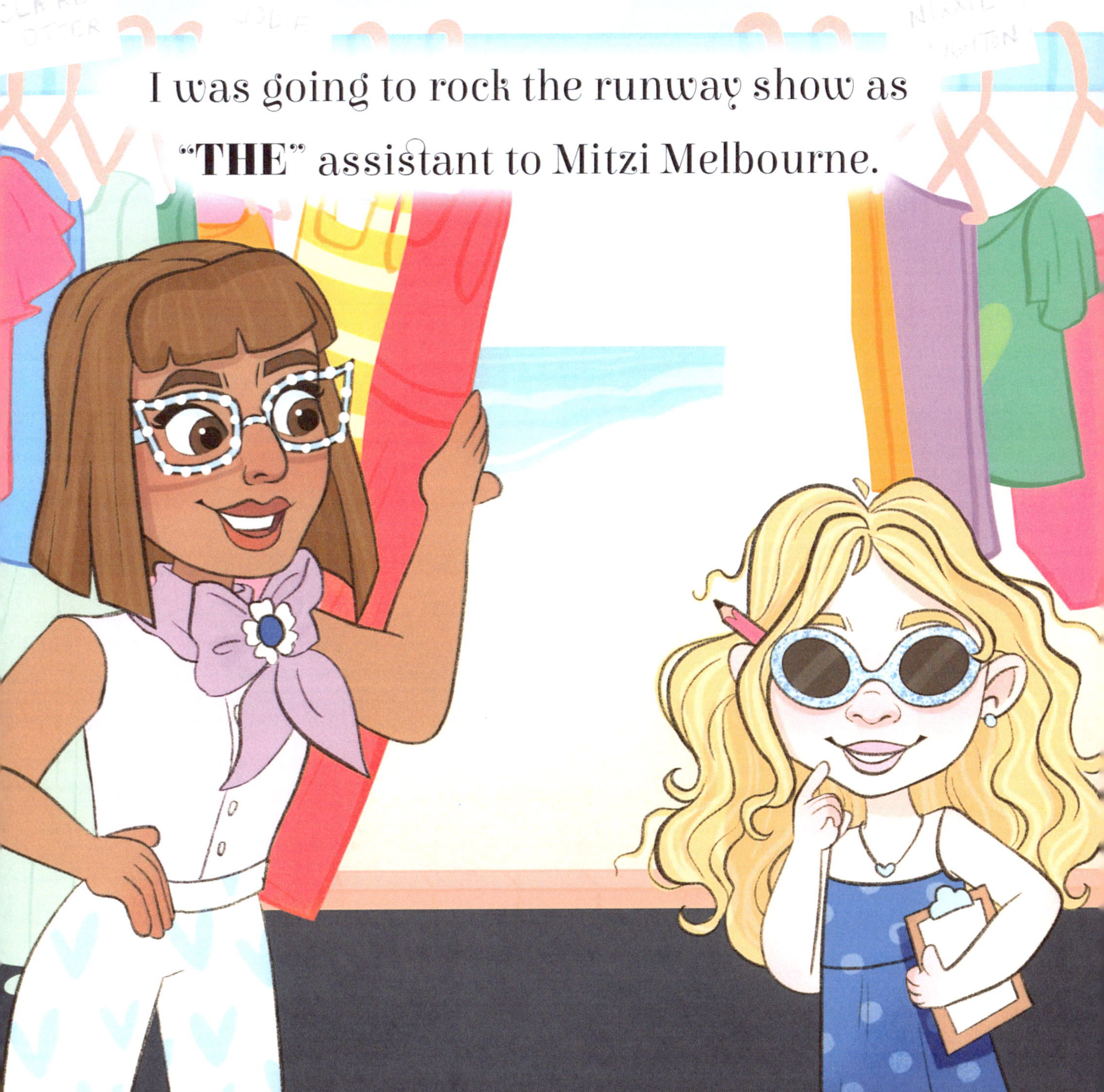

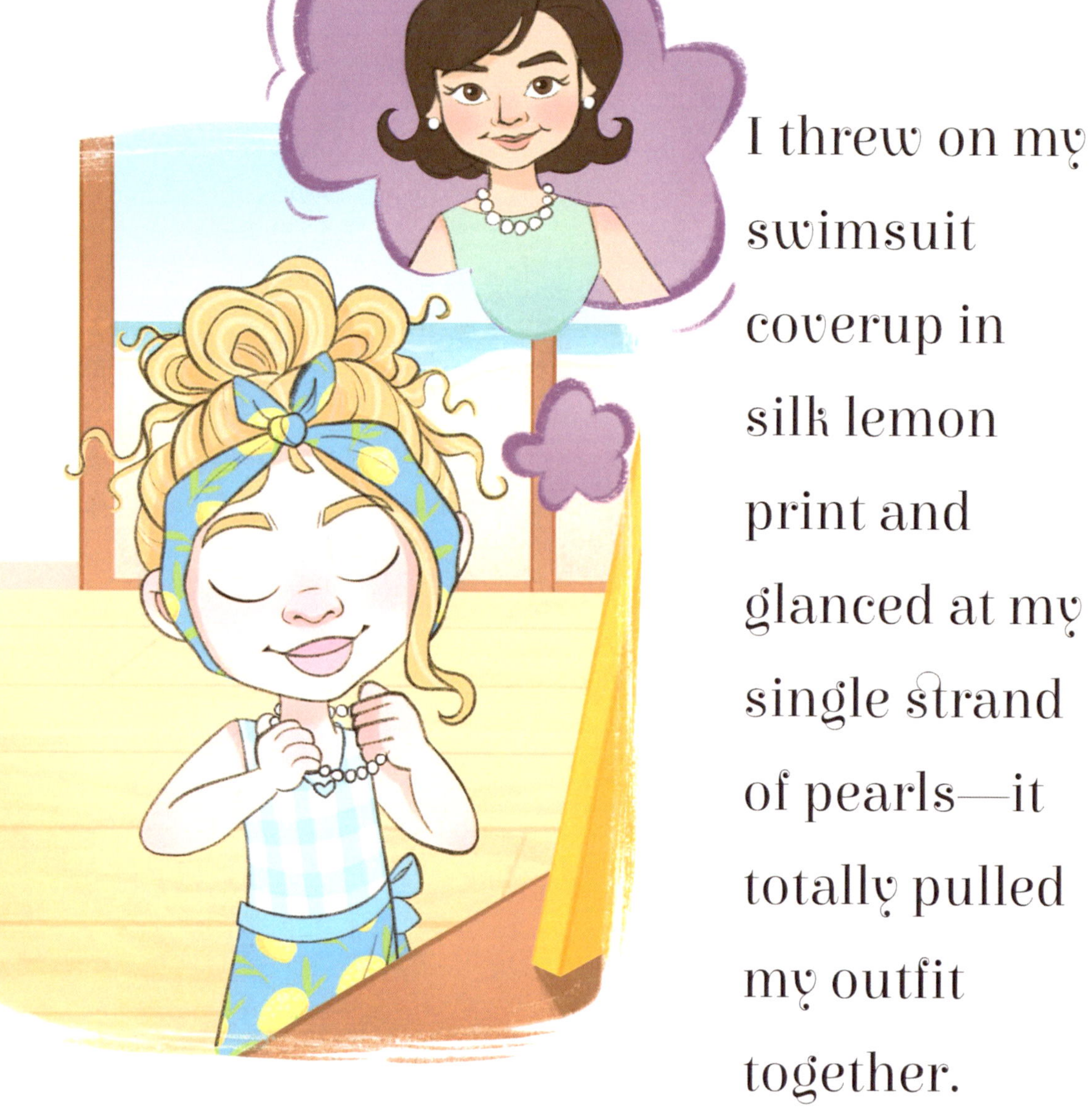

I threw on my swimsuit coverup in silk lemon print and glanced at my single strand of pearls—it totally pulled my outfit together.

Yes, pearls! You know who said "pearls are always appropriate"? The legend fashion icon herself and First Lady, Jaqueline Kennedy Onassis, or "**Jackie O**."

She was so glam and chic! She slept on silk pillowcases, which kept her skin glowing.

Just like Jackie O, I decided to grab my oversized glasses off my head and tie my hair up in a matching silk lemon print scarf. Posh! I had arrived. **Oui, Oui, Mon Chéri!**

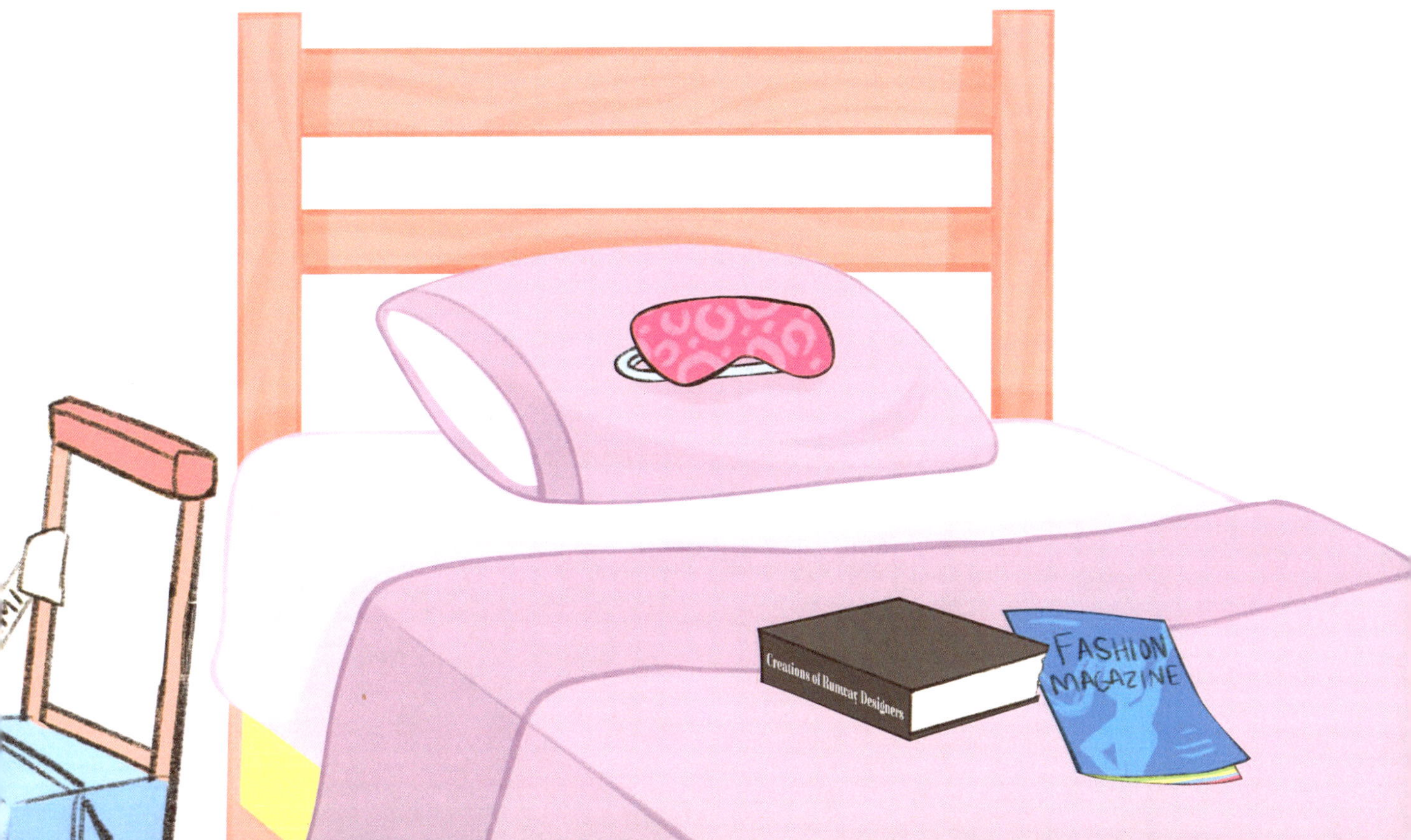

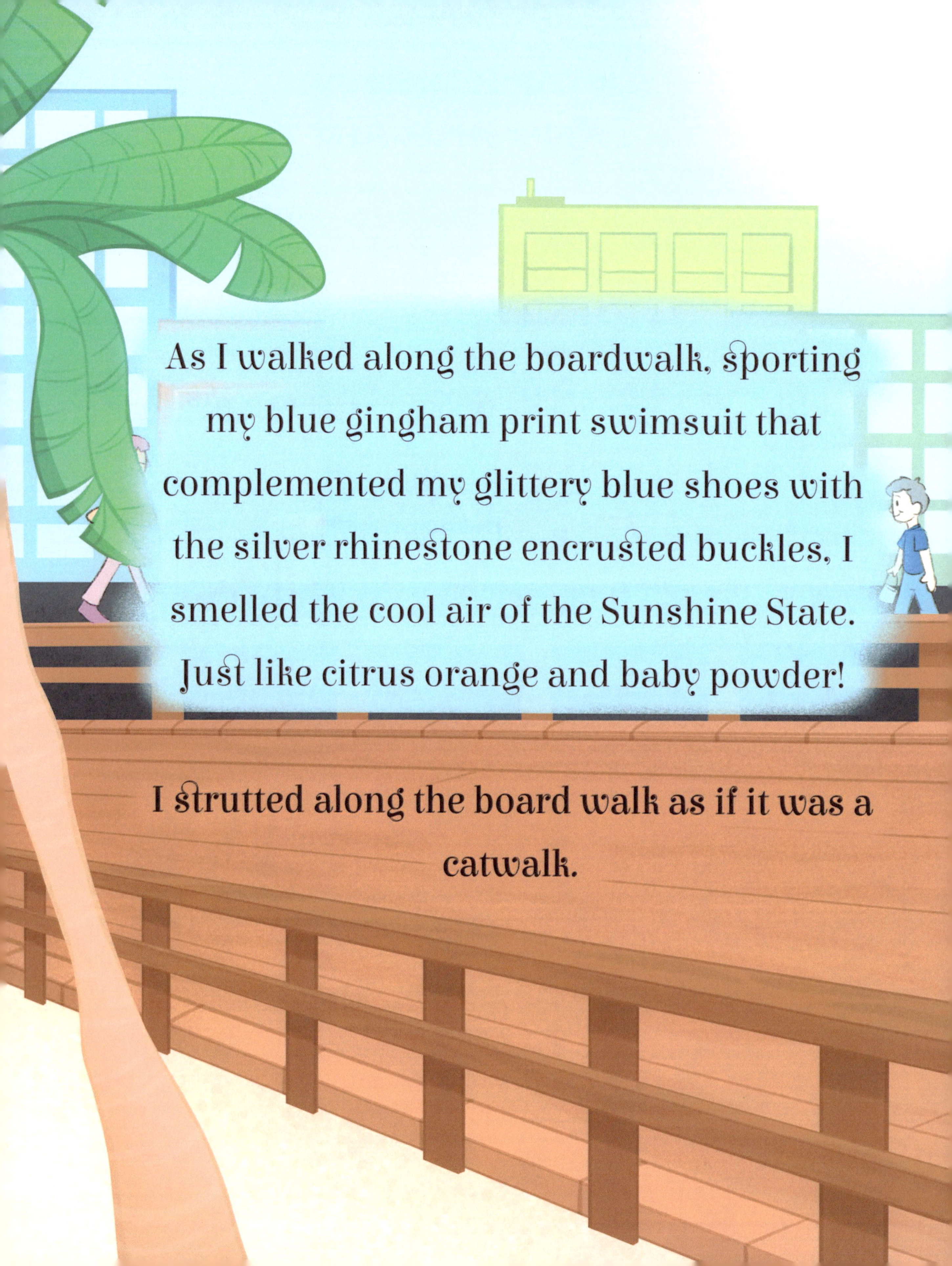

As I walked along the boardwalk, sporting my blue gingham print swimsuit that complemented my glittery blue shoes with the silver rhinestone encrusted buckles, I smelled the cool air of the Sunshine State. Just like citrus orange and baby powder!

I strutted along the board walk as if it was a catwalk.

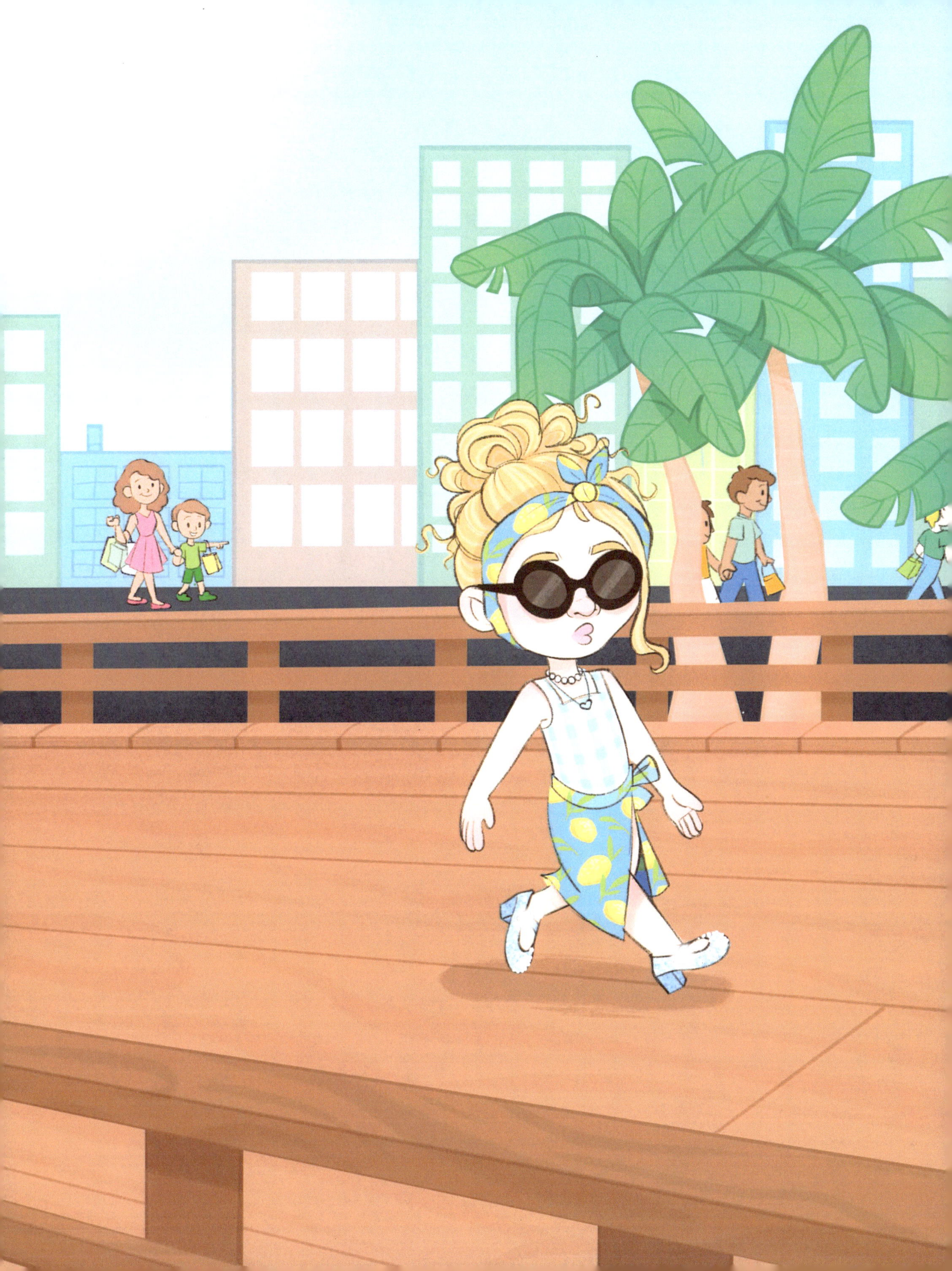

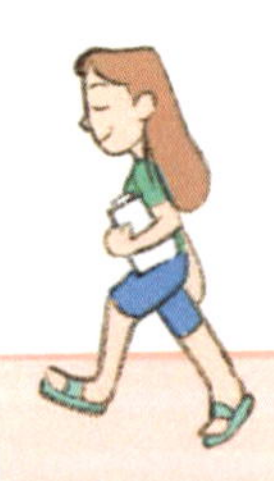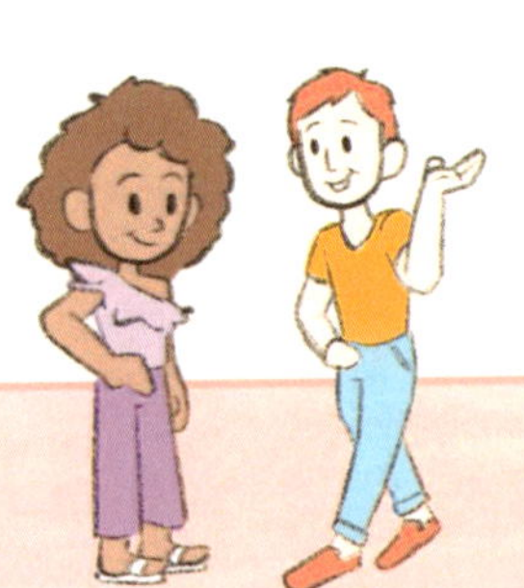

The next day was **Fashion Day**! I walked into a room filled with racks of swimsuits, cover-ups, and resort-wear.

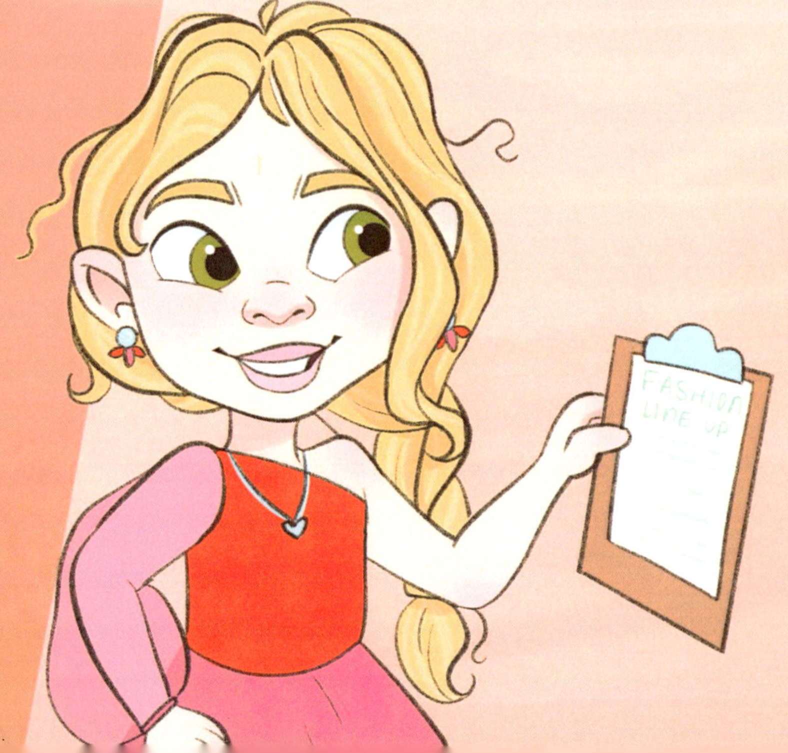

There were also over-the-top glam teams
that all had lipglosses, make-up brushes,
and hair tools at the ready!

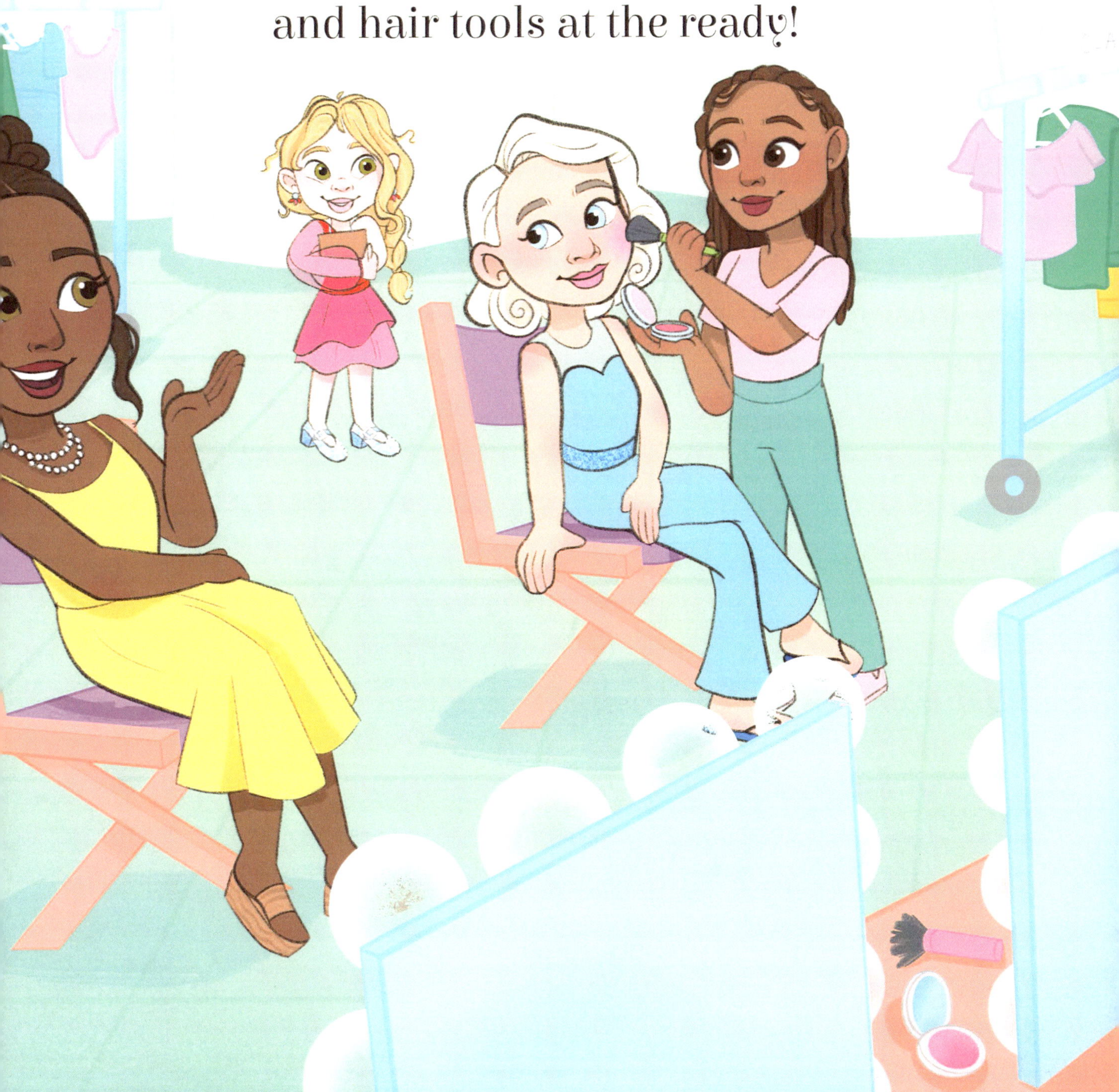

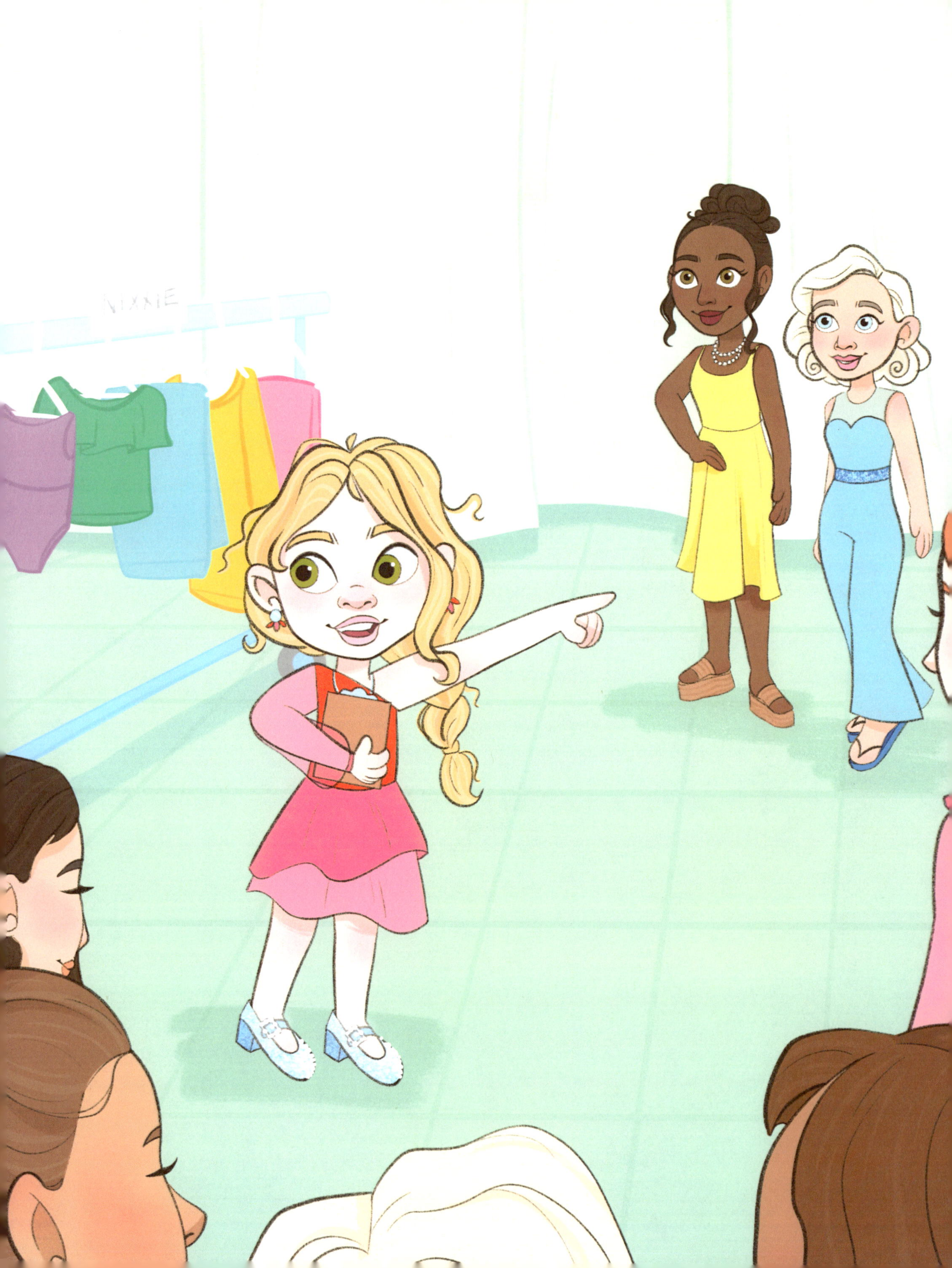

Immediately, I went into "Fashion Action Mode." I put all the models into their line-up.

That is where I met Nixxi Houghton, a model Superstar! Nixxi walked the runway at every big show for every big designer. She was what we call a **"Show Stopper"**—she always closed the show with the "Final Look" on the runway!

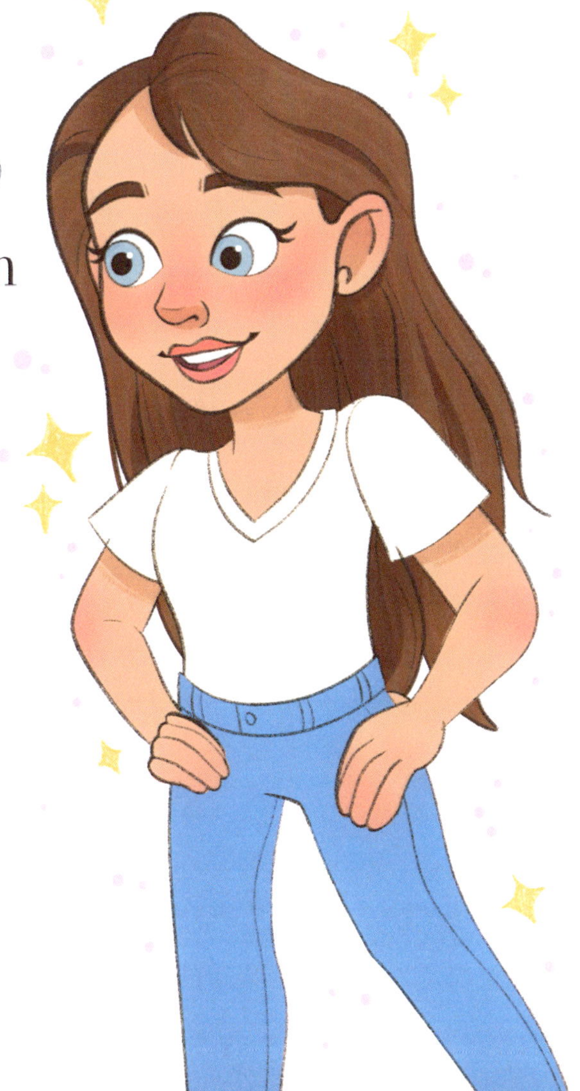

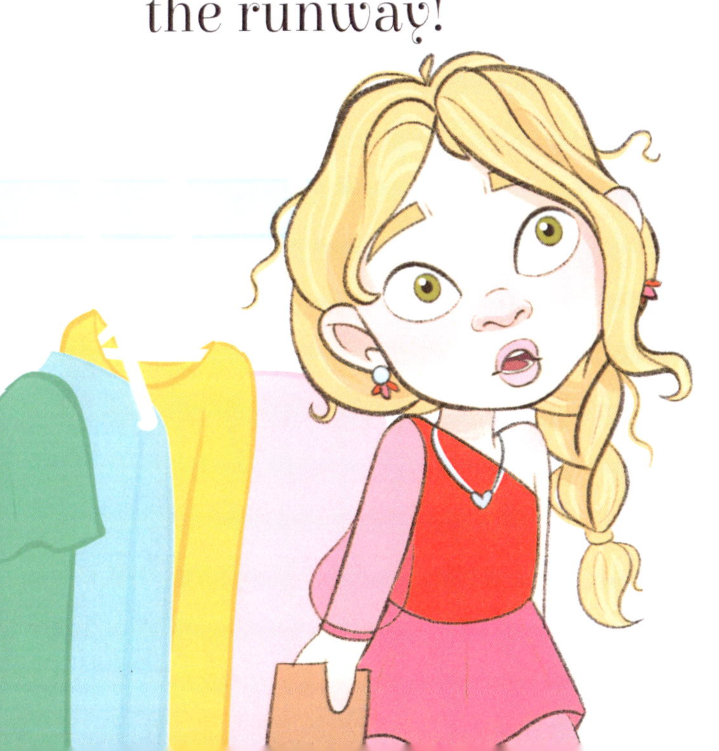

It was my job to make sure things went smoothly and looked effortless as the models glided down the runway. I pulled Nixxi's outfit from the garment rack and handed it to her. I was nervous.

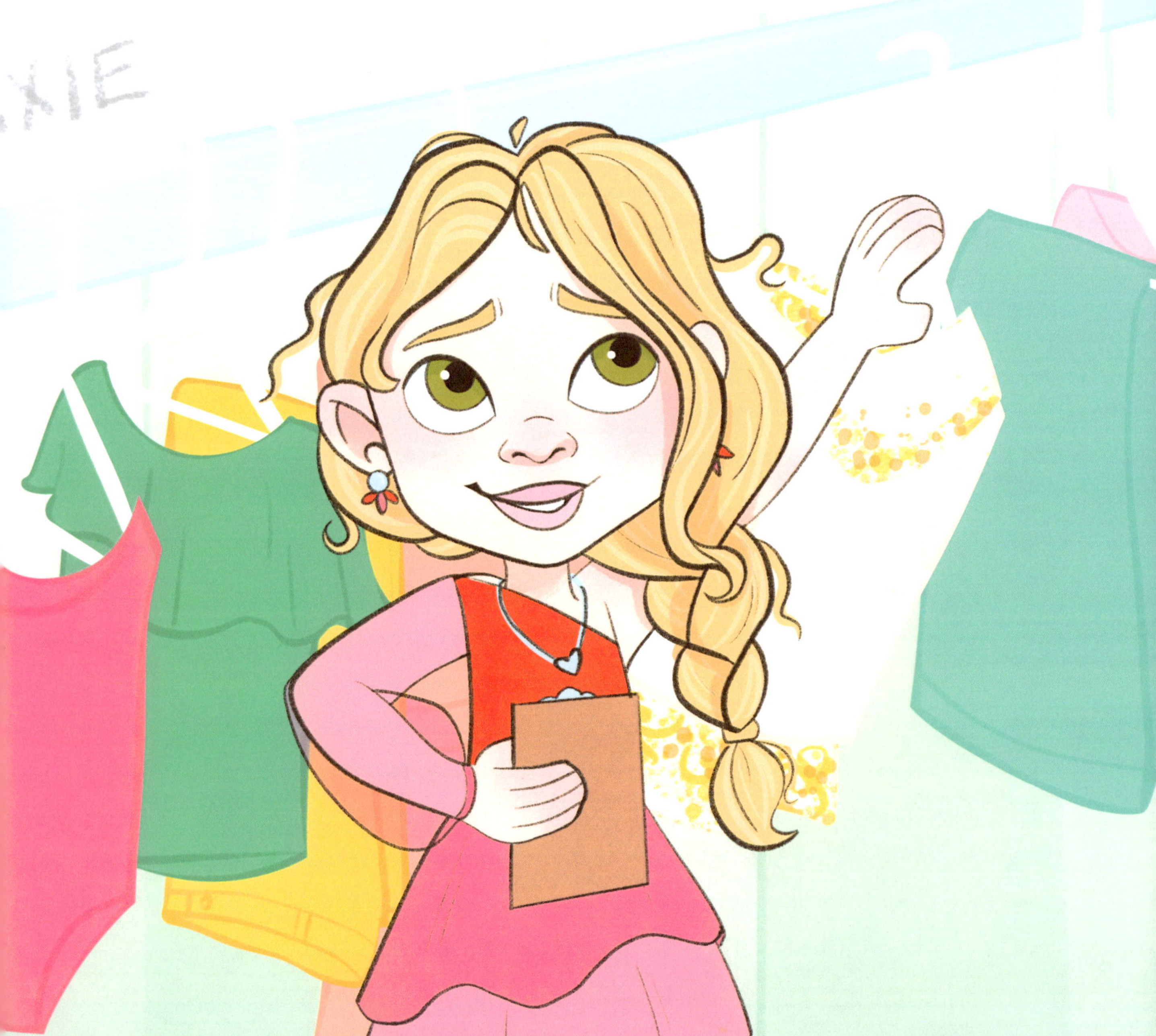

I went to shake her hand. She hugged me and said, "Thank you! I am a hugger." At that moment, I knew we would become fast friends!

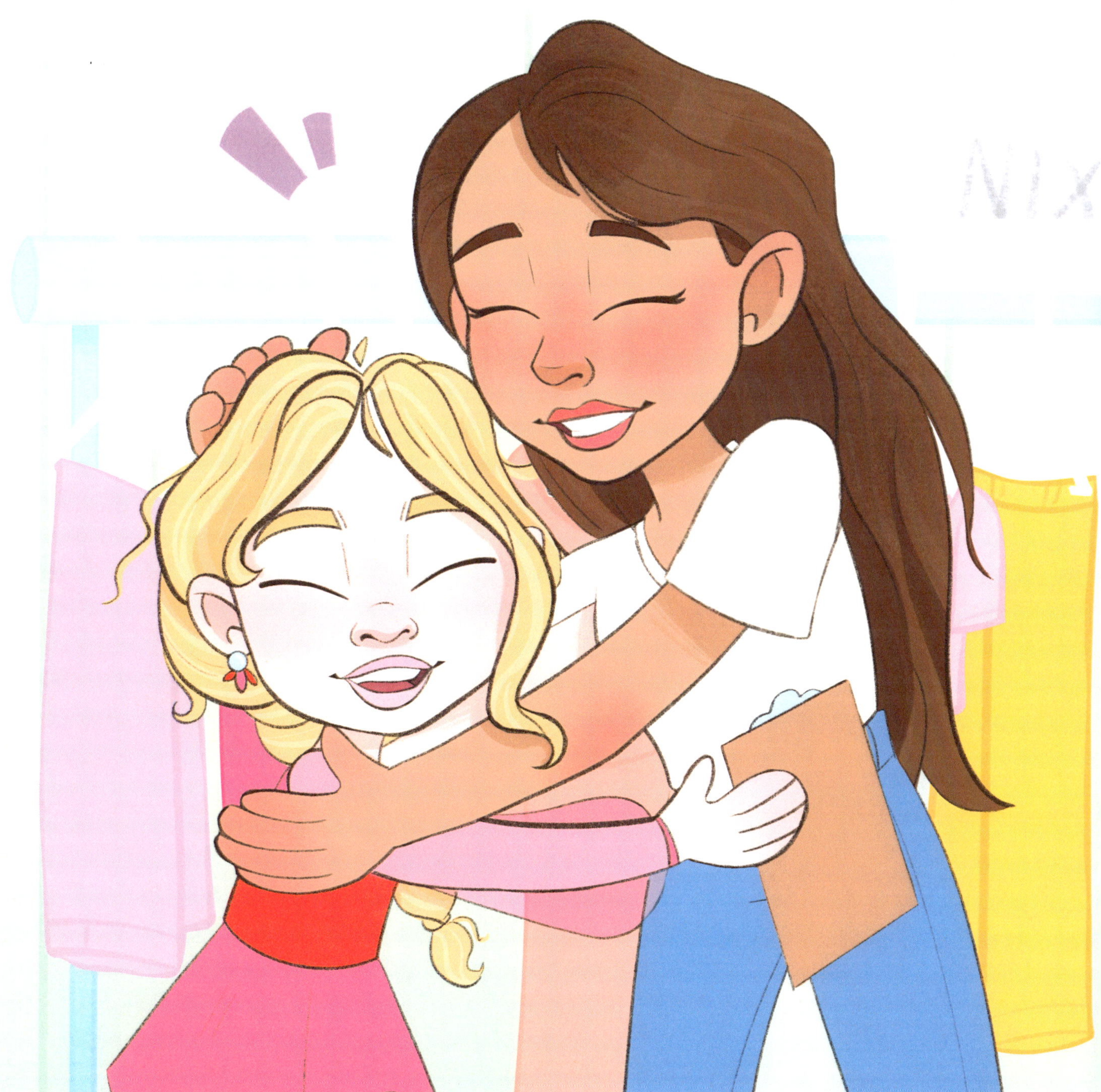

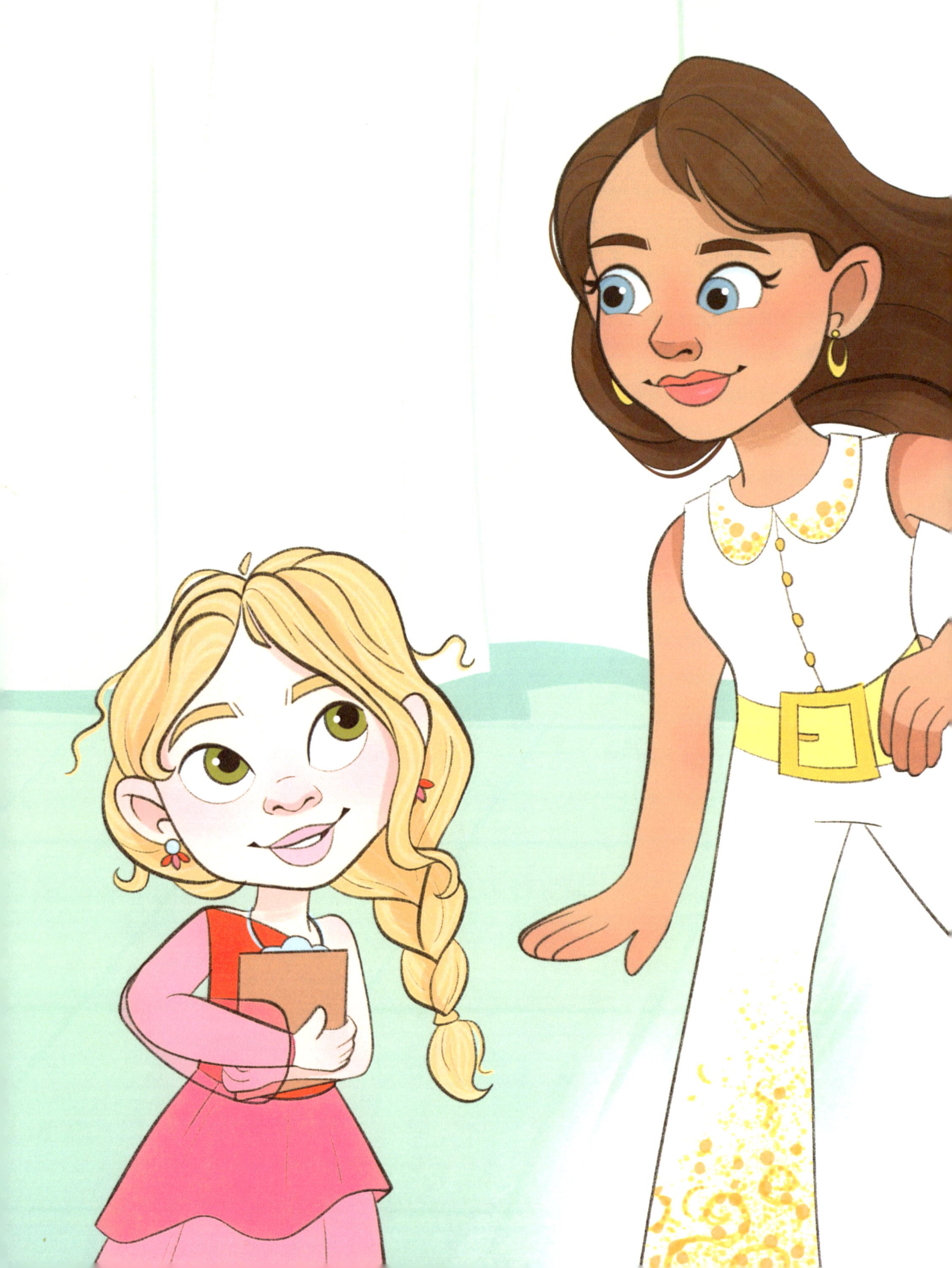

I loved her outfit of choice: **Iconic**!

White flared pants with gold glitter designs. Her matching top was simple—white with a rounded collar with a dust of gold sparkle to tie in the glitter accents of her pants. She paired her outfit with amazing gold strappy sandals. It checked all the boxes for Miami Swim Week.

Oui, Oui, Mon Chéri!

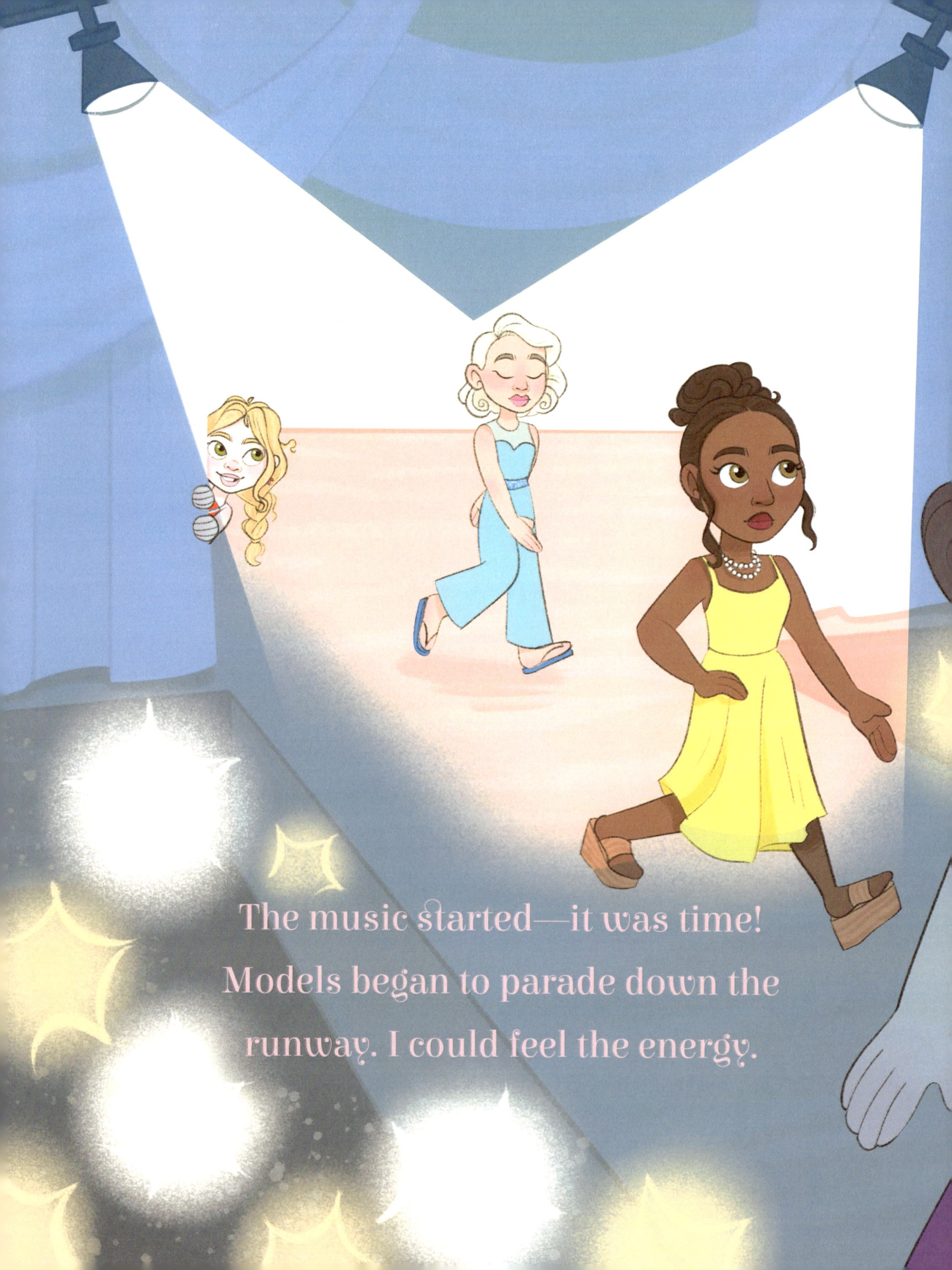

The music started—it was time!
Models began to parade down the
runway. I could feel the energy.

Nixxi yelled, "Farrah!" in an anxious voice,
and I knew something was wrong.

I rushed over, where I saw that the strap
of her sandal had begun to unravel.

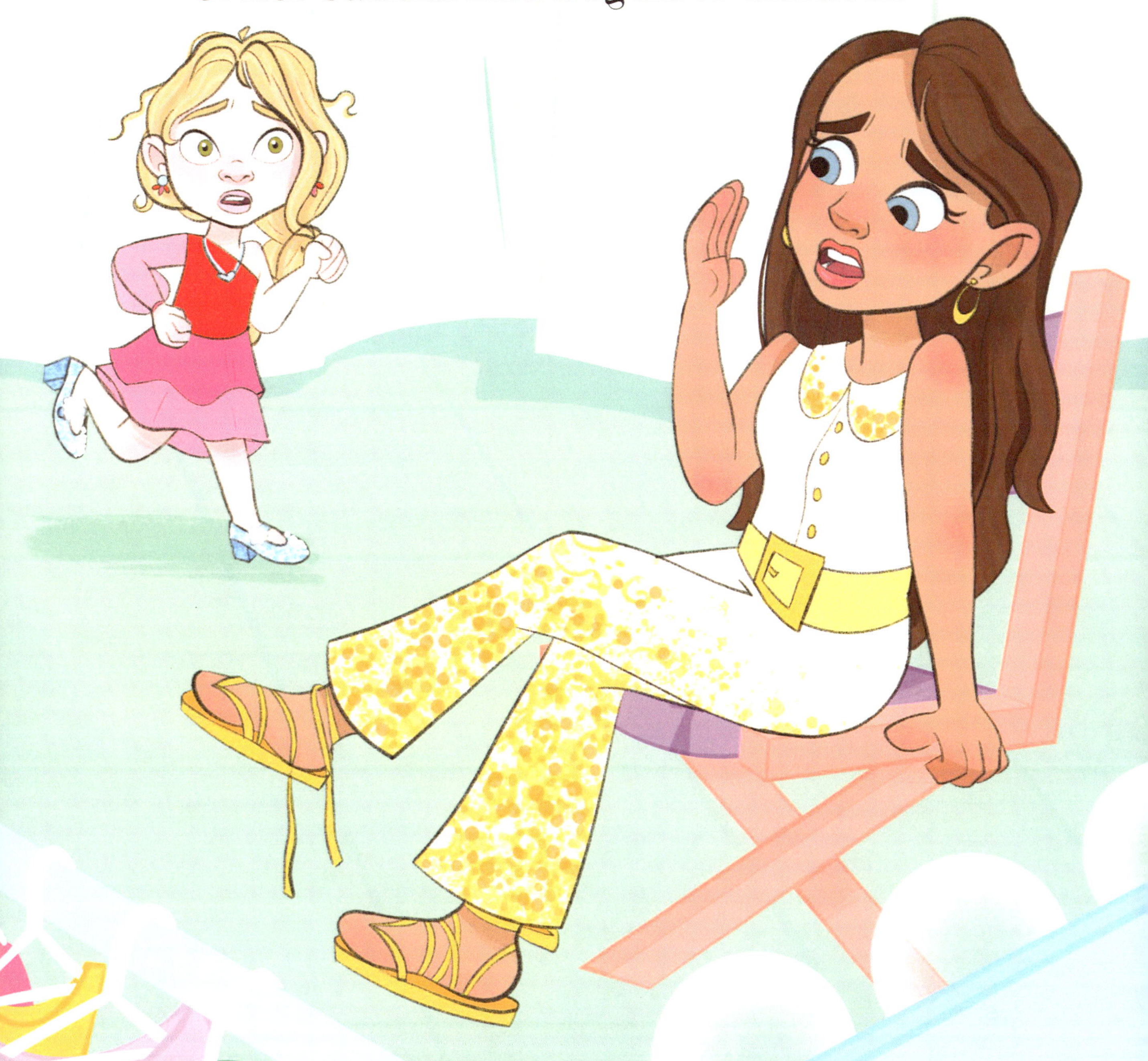

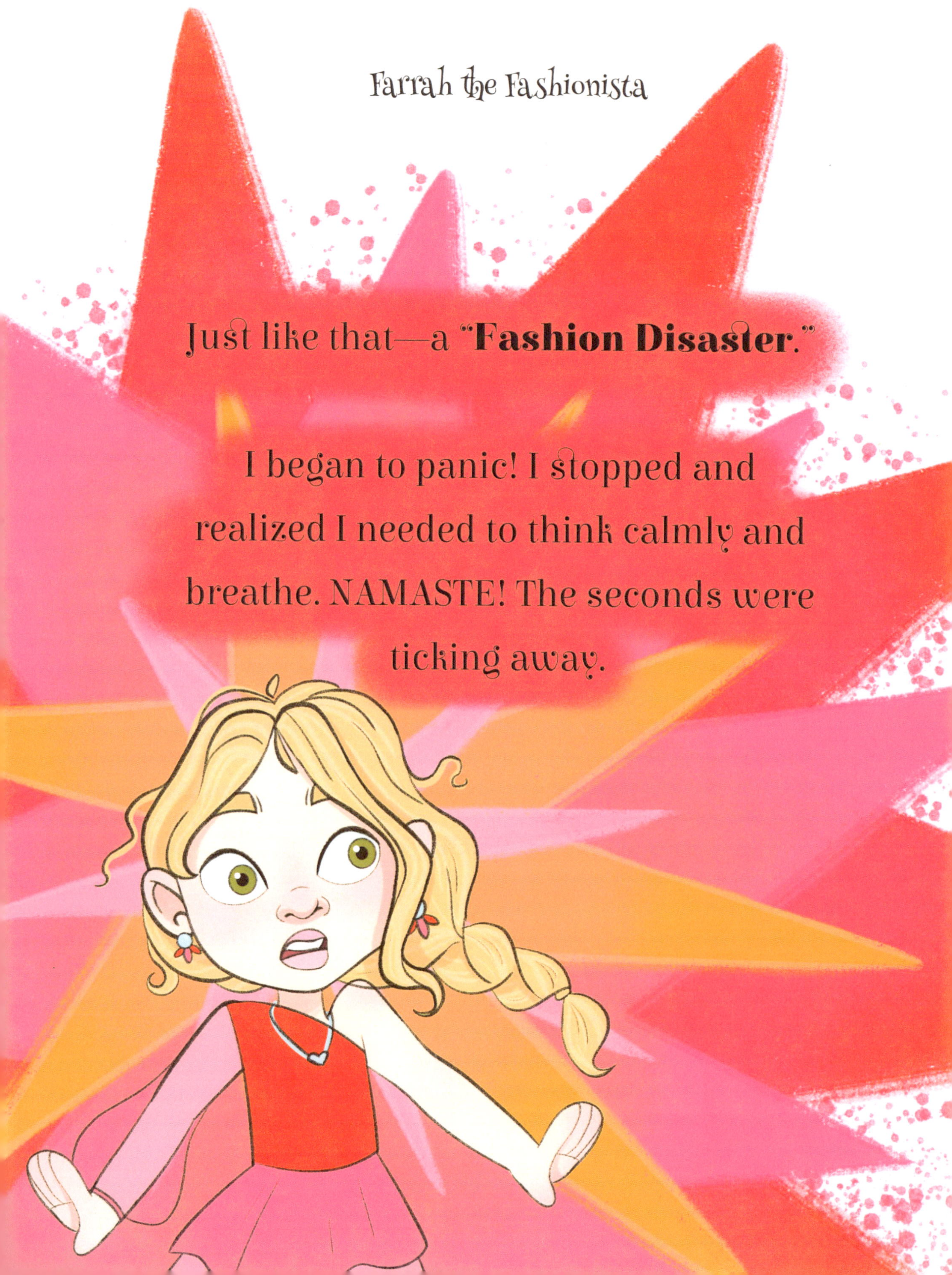

Just like that—a "**Fashion Disaster**."

I began to panic! I stopped and realized I needed to think calmly and breathe. NAMASTE! The seconds were ticking away.

What was I going to do??? Think, Farrah!

Turn the lights off over the runway? **No!**

Send her down the runway in high heels?

No!

Not send Nixxi down the runway? **No way!**

Think! Just then, my energy shifted, and I was focused.

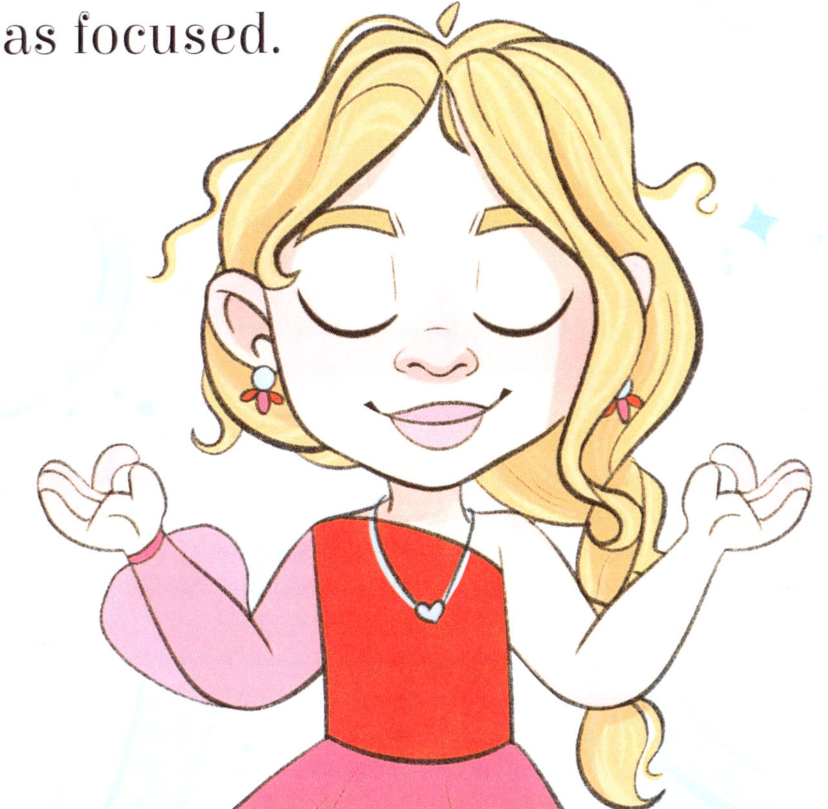

I will cut the straps on the sandals! I pulled out my scissors, closed my eyes, AND...

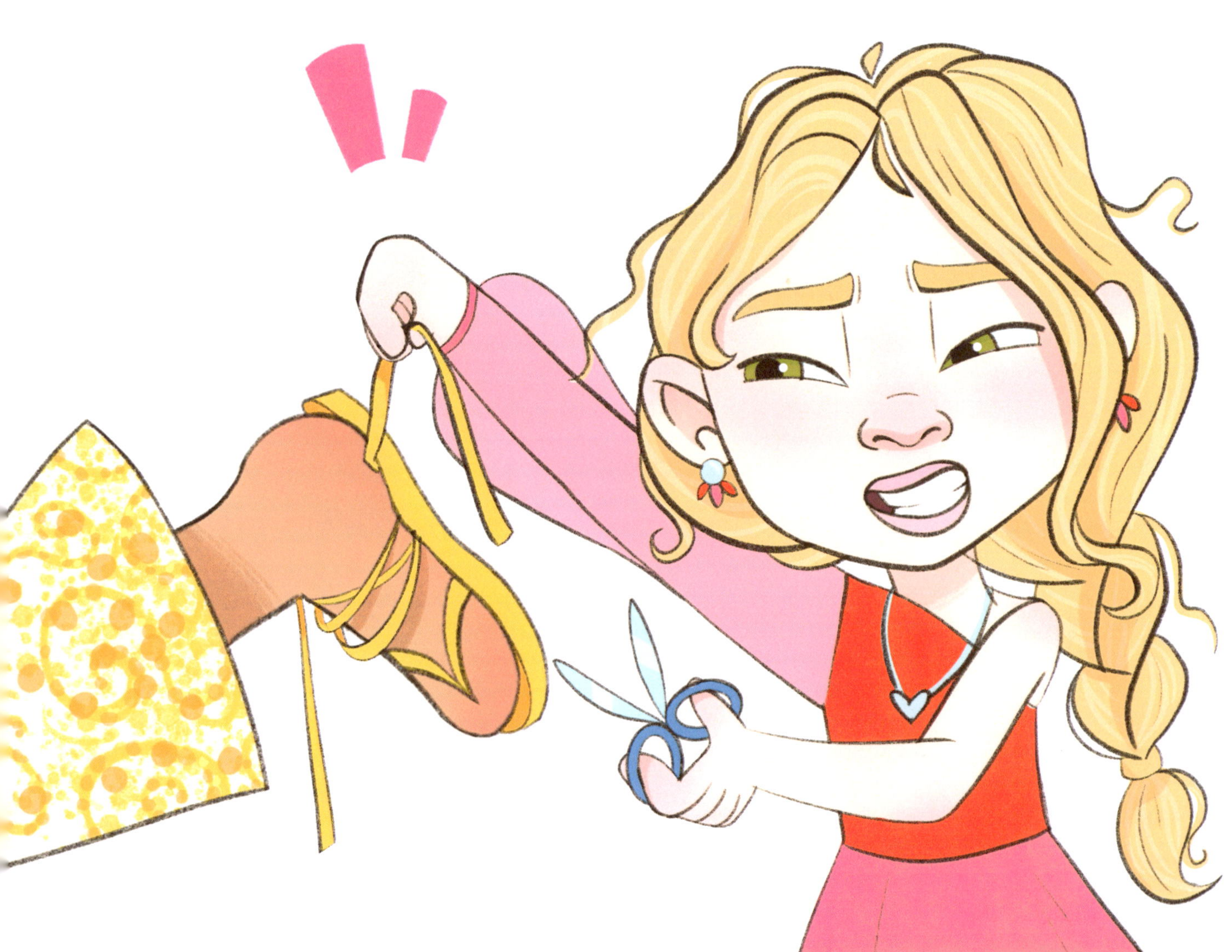

Instant flip flops!

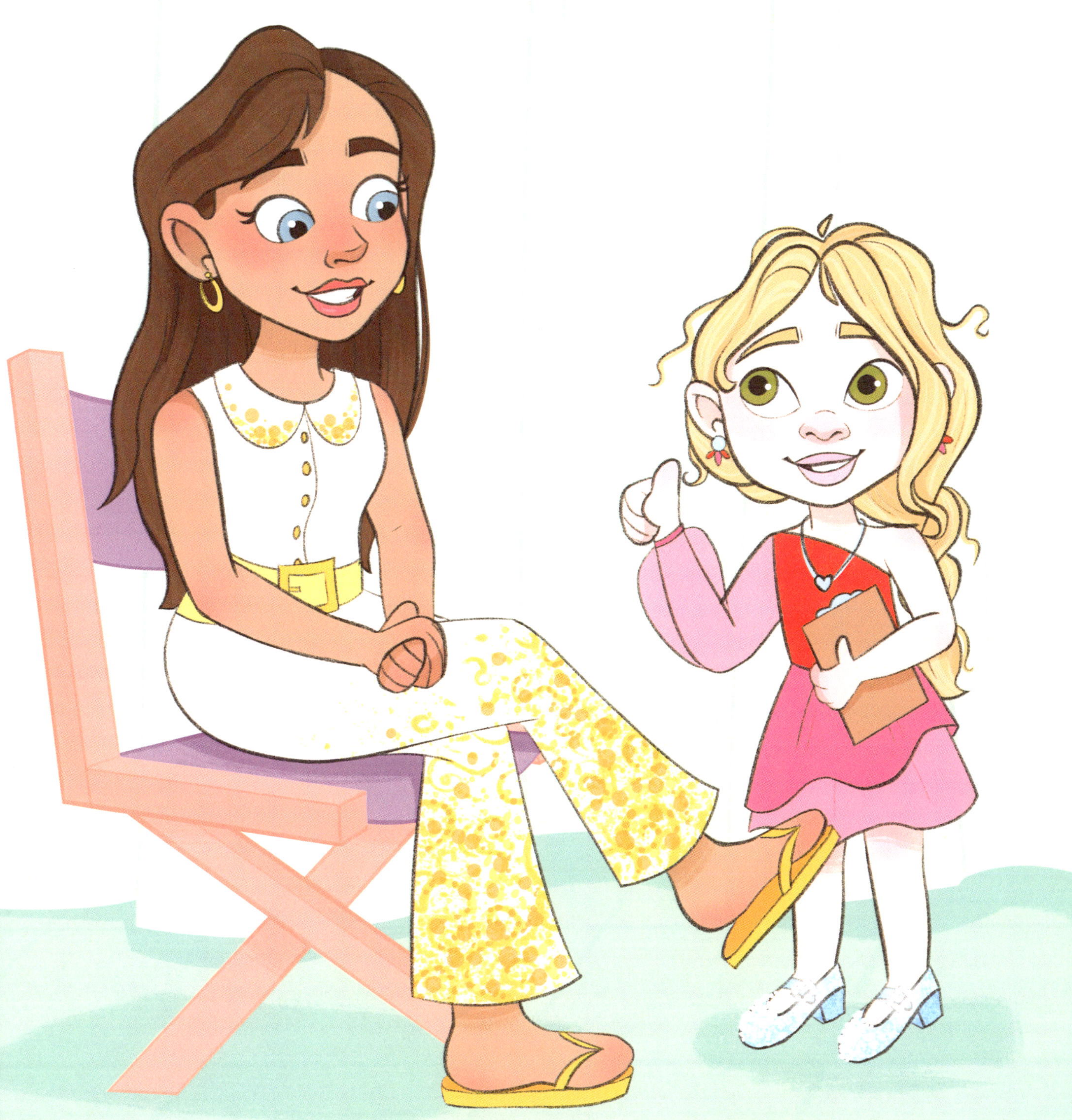

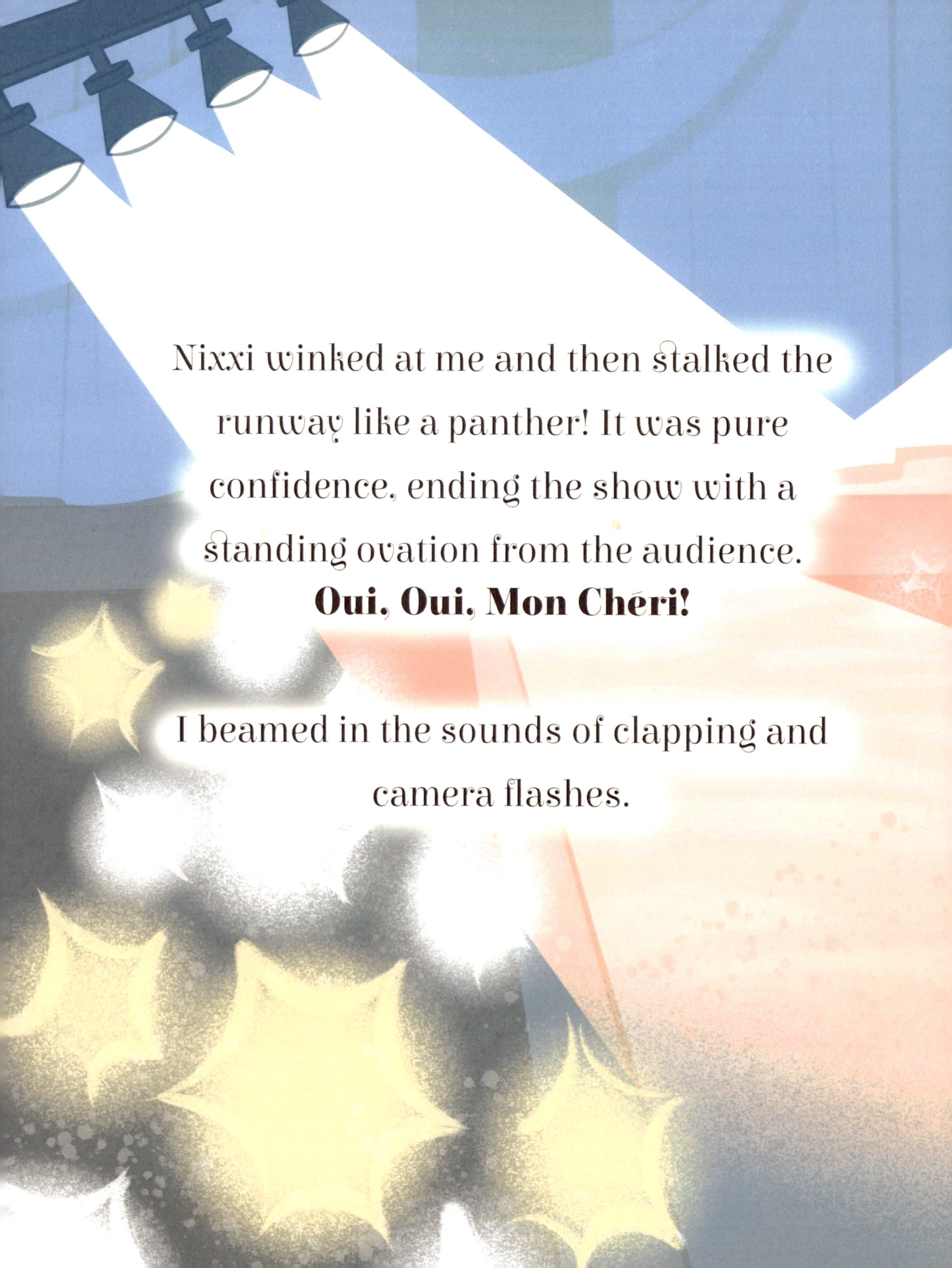

Nixxi winked at me and then stalked the runway like a panther! It was pure confidence, ending the show with a standing ovation from the audience. **Oui, Oui, Mon Chéri!**

I beamed in the sounds of clapping and camera flashes.

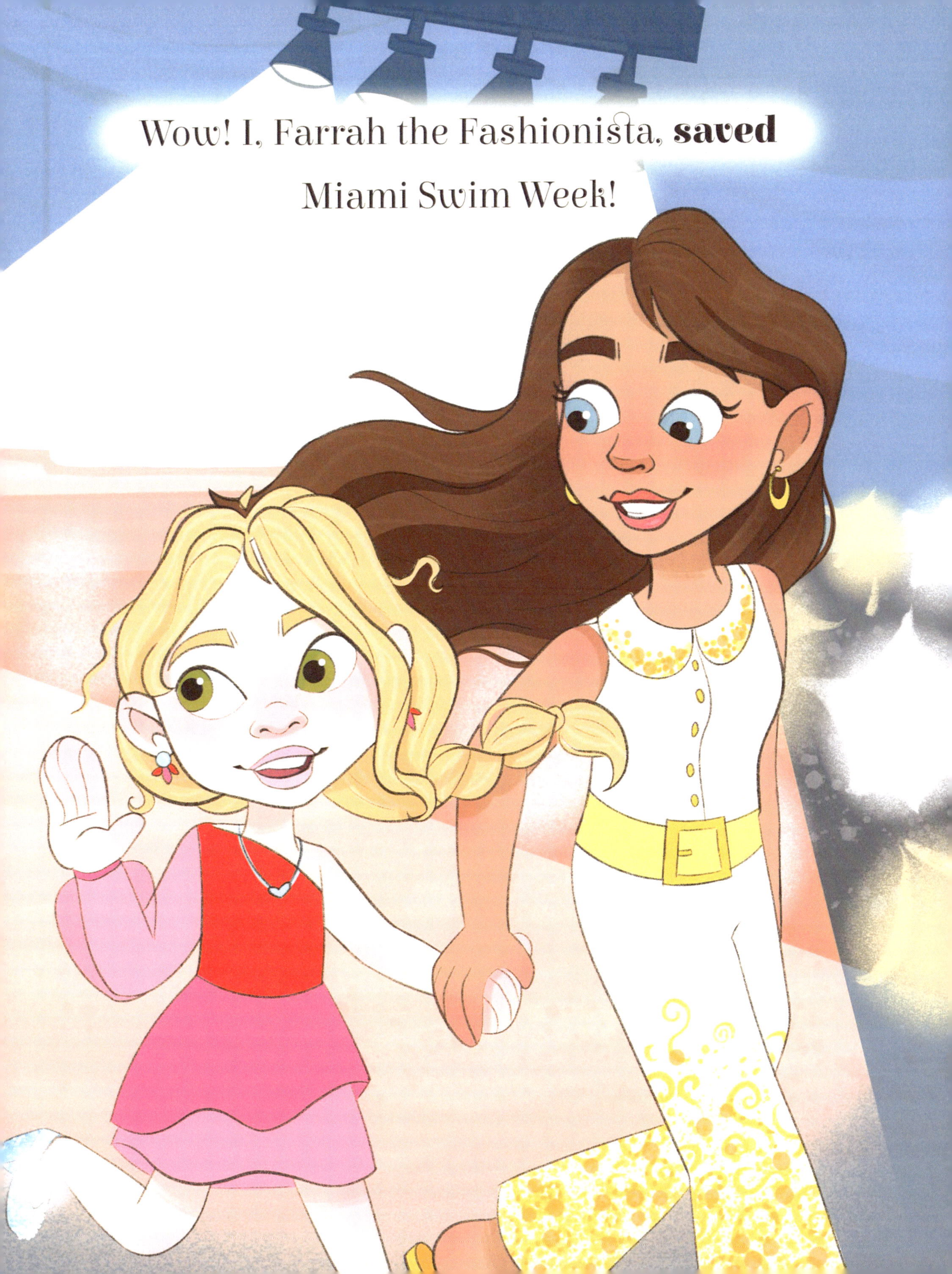

Wow! I, Farrah the Fashionista, **saved**
Miami Swim Week!

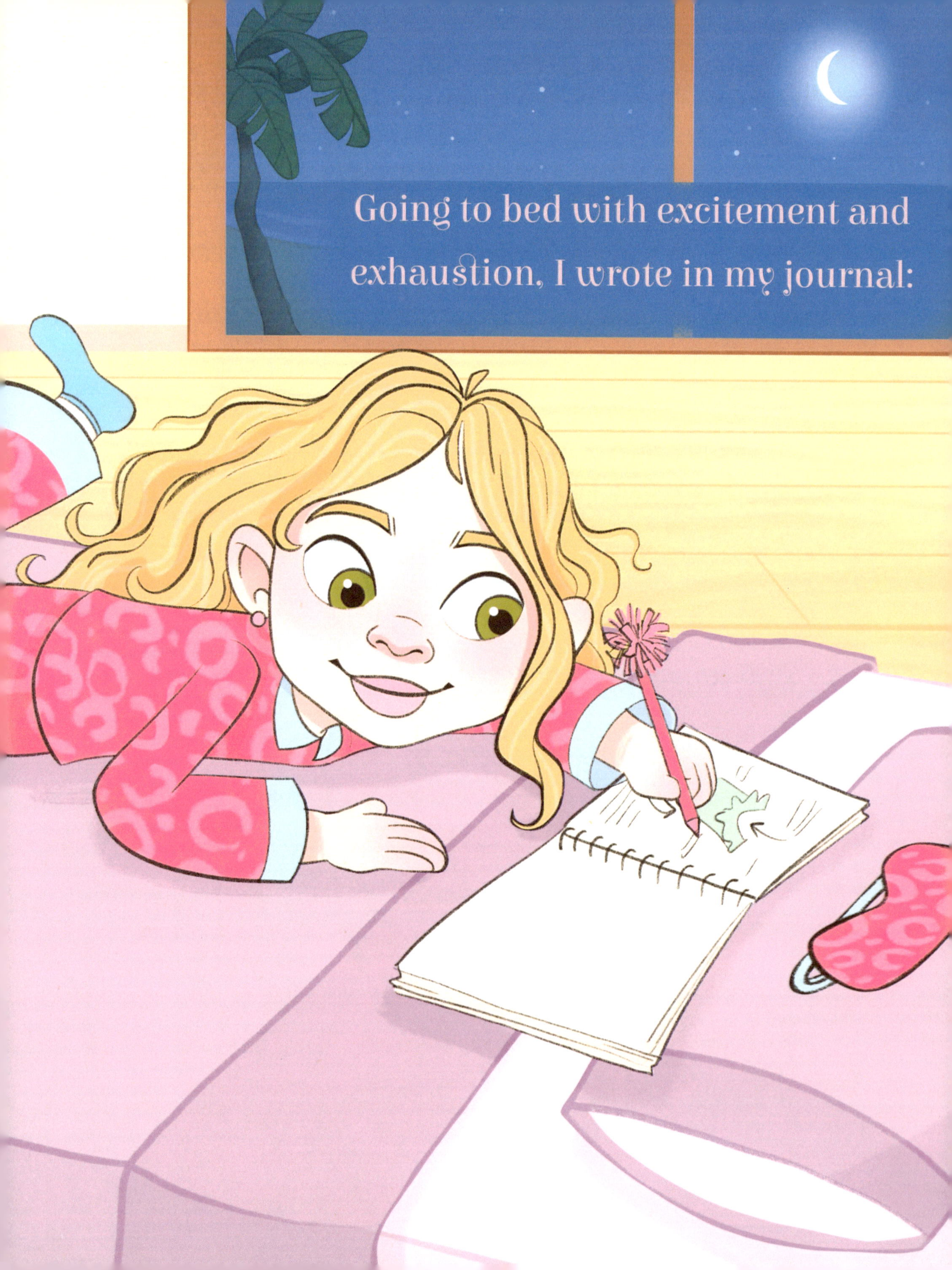
Going to bed with excitement and exhaustion, I wrote in my journal:

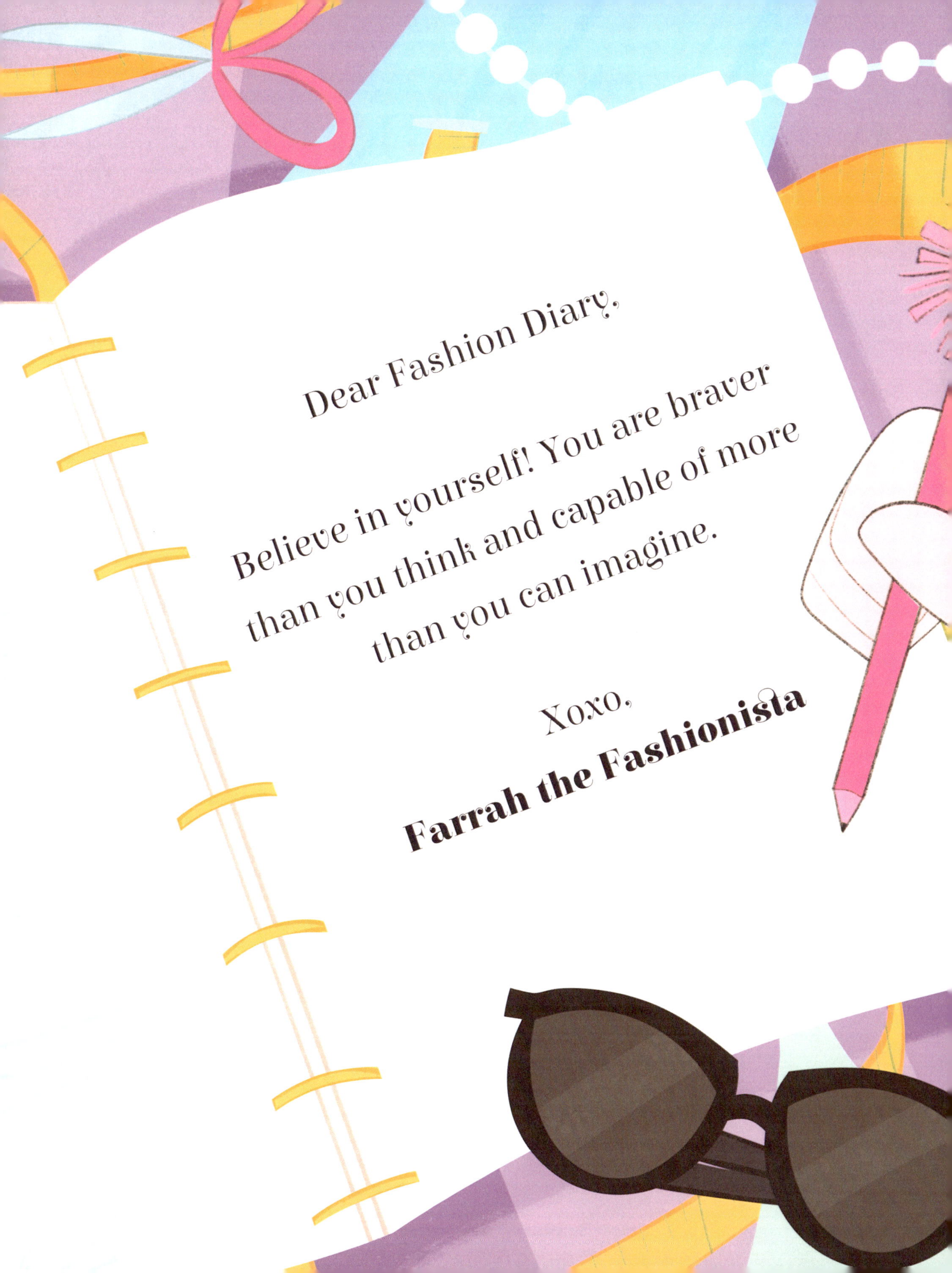

Dear Fashion Diary,

Believe in yourself! You are braver than you think and capable of more than you can imagine.

Xoxo,

Farrah the Fashionista

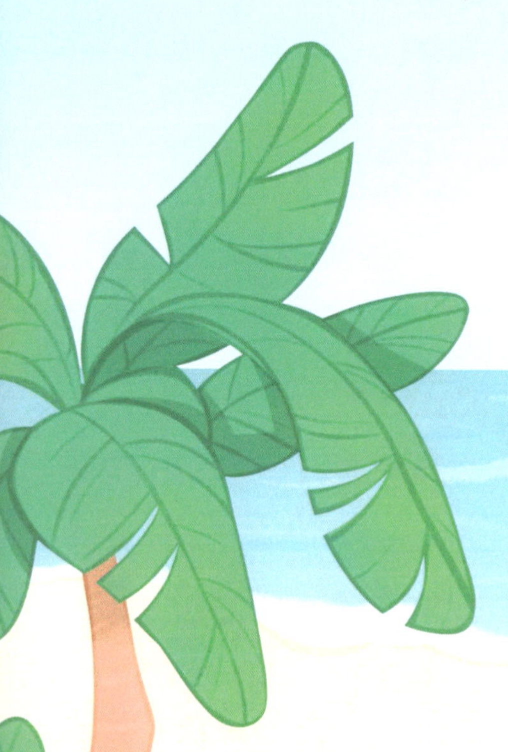
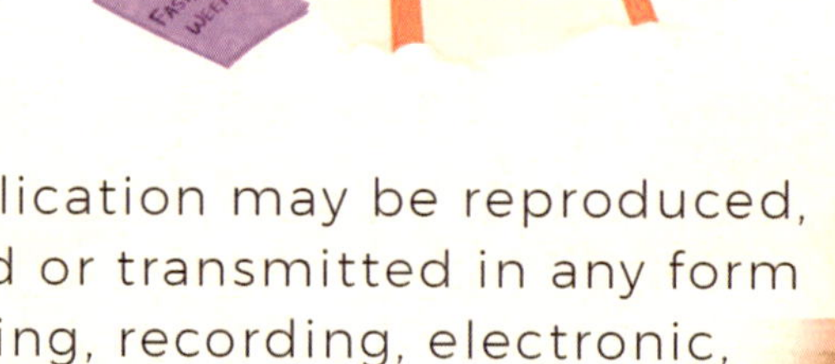